D1361524

CATS
SET III

Korat Cats

Julie Murray
ABDO Publishing Company

visit us at
www.abdopub.com

Published by ABDO Publishing Company, 4940 Viking Drive, Edina, Minnesota 55435.

Printed in the United States.

Photo Credits: Corbis pp. 5, 9, 15, 17, 19; Animals Animals pp. 11, 13, 21;
Peter Arnold p. 7
Contributing Editors: Tamara L. Britton, Kristin Van Cleaf, Stephanie Hedlund
Book Design & Graphics: Neil Klinepier

Library of Congress Cataloging-in-Publication Data

Murray, Julie, 1969-
Korat cats / Julie Murray.
p. cm. -- (Cats. Set III)
Summary: An introduction to the origins, physical characteristics, and behavior of the silver-blue Korat cat, with information on the choosing and care of a Korat kitten.
ISBN 1-57765-864-7
1. Korat cat--Juvenile literature. [1. Korat cat. 2. Cats.] I. Title.

SF449.K67 M87 2002
636.8'2--dc21

2002016387

Contents

Lions, Tigers, and Cats

The first cats lived about 35 million years ago. There are several different types of cats. But they all belong to the animal family **Felidae**. There are 38 different species in this family.

Cats are organized into three different categories. Examples of big cats are lions, tigers, jaguars, and leopards. The small cats include **domestic** cats, lynx, and bobcats. Cheetahs are in a group by themselves.

Domestic cats are believed to be the ancestors of the African wildcat. They were tamed about 4,000 years ago in Egypt. Today, there are more than 40 different recognized **breeds** of domestic cats.

The jaguar is a big cat that roars. Small cats purr. This is one difference between the categories.

Korat Cats

For hundreds of years, Korat cats have been prized in Thailand. They were written about in the *Cat Book of Poems*. This ancient book was written between A.D. 1350 and 1767. It is now held in the Bangkok National Library.

Korats are named for the **province** of Khorat, Thailand. There they are seen as a symbol of **prosperity**. Korats are often given to **newlyweds** and important people as lucky charms.

In 1959, the Korat **breed** came to the United States. That year, an American diplomat in Thailand received a pair of Korats. He sent the cats to Mrs. Jean Johnson in Oregon.

In 1966, Korats were recognized as an official breed. Today, Korats are rare all over the world, even in their native Thailand.

Korat cats are believed to be lucky and are treated as very special creatures. Because of this, they expect the best possible care!

Qualities

Korats have strong personalities. They are affectionate with their owners. But these cats don't always like strangers. Sometimes they even hiss at them.

Intelligence is one quality of Korat cats. They can be taught to walk on a leash and do tricks. These cats are also very playful and active. But if not given the proper attention, Korats can be demanding and stubborn.

Loyalty is another Korat quality. They are friendly and loving. They prefer to live in a quiet, calm atmosphere. A house with lots of activity and noise is not for them. Korats have a pleasant voice and sometimes can be quite vocal.

Korats like to play, especially if you are playing with them. Korats will play fetch and do other tricks.

Coat and Color

Korats have a short, glossy coat. It lies close to the skin because it does not have an **undercoat**. The fine hair feels satiny to the touch.

Korat cats are silver-blue all over. The tips of their hairs have a silvery sheen. This gives the impression that Korats have **halos**. Where the hair is shorter, the silvery color stands out.

In Europe, Korats with lilac color have been **bred**. But this form of the breed may not be accepted in the United States for competitions.

Bright green eyes are one feature of Korats. Kittens may have amber or yellow eyes. This color slowly changes over the first two years of their life. Korats look much like Russian Blue cats.

Korats have a heart-shaped face. The heart starts at the cat's chin, goes to the tips of the ears, and then down to the top of its head.

Size

Korats are medium-sized cats. Their bodies are lean, limber, and muscular. Korats often weigh more than they appear to.

This **breed** has a slightly curved back and a wide chest. Korats' front legs tend to be shorter than their back legs. Their tails are heavier at the base and taper to a round tip.

Korats have a heart-shaped head. Their ears are wide at the base and rounded at the tips. They sit high on the Korat's head. Korats' eyes look oversized on their face. They are large and set far apart.

The compact body of the Korat is deceiving!
This breed is often much heavier than it appears.

Care

All cats keep themselves clean. They do this by licking their fur often. Because of this and their short coat, Korats are easy to groom. Brushing them once a week with a rubber brush will remove loose hairs.

Like all cats, Korats will frequently need to sharpen their claws. This is a natural behavior for cats. Providing them with a scratching post will save your furniture from damage.

All cats love to play. Movement is important for their enjoyment. So provide them with toys that they can move. There are many different cat toys available today. A ball, **catnip** mouse, or anything they can move with their paws will be good.

It is a natural instinct for cats to bury their waste. So they should be trained to use a **litter box**. The litter box needs to be cleaned every day. Cats should also be **spayed** or **neutered** unless you are planning on **breeding** them.

Korats enjoy playing. Providing your cat with a hideout is one way to entertain it.

Feeding

All cats are **carnivores**. They require food that is high in protein, such as meat or fish. Cats can be very picky and do not like changes in their diet.

Homemade diets usually do not provide the **nutrients** that cats need. A better choice is commercial cat food. It comes in three types. They are dry, semidry, and canned. Each offers similar nutritional value.

Dry foods are the most convenient. They can prevent **tartar** buildup on your cat's teeth. Canned foods are the most appealing to cats. But they do not stay fresh for very long.

Cats also need fresh water every day. Your cat may love to drink milk. But many cats are unable to **digest** milk. It will often make them sick. Cats also love treats. You can find a variety of treats at your local pet store.

Kittens will drink their mother's milk for about eight weeks.

Kittens

Baby cats are called kittens. Cats are **pregnant** for about 65 days before the kittens are born. A Korat usually has a **litter** of four or five kittens.

All kittens are born blind and helpless. They need to drink their mother's milk for the first three weeks. Then they start to eat solid food. Most kittens stop drinking their mother's milk when they are about eight weeks old.

Kittens start becoming independent when they are about three weeks old. By then they can see, hear, and stand on their own. At about seven weeks, they can run and play. When kittens are 12 weeks old, they can be sold or given away.

All kittens are born with blue eyes. A Korat's eye color changes to yellow or amber, then to green.

Buying a Kitten

A healthy cat will live about 14 to 16 years. A kitten will become very attached to its owner. So before you buy a kitten, be sure you will be able to take care of it for as long as it lives.

There are many places to get a kitten. A qualified **breeder** is the best place to buy a **purebred** kitten. When buying from a breeder, be sure to get the kitten's **pedigree** papers and health records. Pet shelters, veterinarians, and cat shows are also good places to find a kitten.

When choosing a kitten, check to see that it is healthy. Its ears, nose, mouth, and fur should all be clean. Its eyes should be bright and clear. The kitten should be alert and playful in its surroundings.

Your cat will need to visit
a veterinarian regularly.
The vet will help your
cat stay healthy!

Glossary

breed - a group of cats that shares the same appearance and characteristics. A breeder is a person who raises cats. Raising cats is often called breeding them.

carnivore - an animal or plant that eats meat.

catnip - the dried leaves and stems of a plant in the mint family. Catnip is used as a stuffing in cat toys because some cats are attracted to its strong smell.

digest - to break down food in the stomach.

domestic - animals that are tame.

Felidae - the Latin name for the cat family.

halo - a circle of light appearing to surround an object.

litter - all of the kittens born at one time to a mother cat.

litter box - a box where cats dispose of their waste.

neuter - to remove a male animal's reproductive organs.

newlyweds - a man and woman just married.

nutrients - vitamins and minerals that all living things need to survive.

pedigree - a record of an animal's ancestors.

pregnant - having one or more babies growing within the body.

prosperity - the condition of being successful or thriving.

province - a main division of a country.

purebred - an animal whose parents are both from the same breed.

spay - to remove a female animal's reproductive organs.

tartar - a crust that forms on the teeth. Tartar is made of saliva, food particles, and salts.

undercoat - soft, short hair or fur that is partly covered by longer protective hairs.

Web Sites

Would you like to learn more about Korat cats? Please visit **www.abdopub.com** to find up-to-date Web site links to more information on the Korat breed. These links are routinely monitored and updated to provide the most current information available.

Index

4/04